Remember to Harvest

Remember to Harvest

Joey Doherty

Dedication

This is for those who keep me curious. Whether you walk on two legs or twelve. Whether you grew in a womb or the dirt. You are family and you are appreciated.

Full Circle

For every book sold, a tree will be planted through the organization, Trees for the Future. A tree was cut down to bring this book to life, so the least I can do is replace it. After all, many of the words within these pages were inspired by nature.

Contents

Remember to Harvest

Harvesting Authenticity

I'd Rather

I'd rather love fiercely and break totally,
than never know love.

I'd rather frowns exist,
than have meaningless smiles.

I'd rather talk less,
so I can feel more.

I'd rather do less,
so I can be more.

I'd rather live truth alone,
than live false with others.

I'd rather search without ever knowing for sure,
than be given one truth.

I'd rather walk slowly,
so I can observe that much more of life.

I'd rather thorns exist,
so the rose means that much more.

I'd rather live vulnerable and free,
than safe and imprisoned.

I'd rather trust in everything,
so I can trust in myself.

In Her Likeness

You know that first leaf to fall each autumn?
I bet you can be just as brave.

You know that blazing Sun?
I bet you can wear the same passion.

You know the spider web that pulls you off the trail?
I bet you can be just as captivating.

You know that sturdy oak tree?
I bet you can be just as confident.

You know the Moon that never stays the same?
I bet you can make change look just as beautiful.

Sun to Human

Our resemblance is there when you smile.
Smile more.

I'blush when you admire me from millions of miles
away.
Admire more.

You're happy when you cultivate your passions.
Cultivate more.

You're kind when you notice the smallest acorn.
Notice more.

You're living when you love.
Love more.

You're unstoppable when you realize your potential.
Realize more.

You're inspiring when you speak from your core.
Speak it more.

Unsure and Proud

Let's talk
and start with one question,
but leave with many.

Let's be unsure.
Let's be scared.
Let's be real.

Let's not let the safety of answers
take away from the life
they'll never know.

Lead the Way

Curiosity is my favorite compass.

It doesn't point toward right.
It doesn't point toward wrong.

It just points toward living.

Take me there.

They are a Gift

So many types of truth.
So many conversations to have
that aren't forced.

You know those people
who bring out your shy soul
and allow whatever comes,
to be?

They are a gift.

Whatever and
whenever and
whoever you need to be,
it's good.

Ancestors of Now

What if your ancestors were sitting across from you?
Those ancestors too ancient for the history books.

Their language would have no resemblance to your own.
They're from a time with no verbal communication.

But their mannerisms.
Oh, that unspoken language
could reach further than any word.

Their gestures were art.
Unexplainably intricate and expressive.
Showing their true selves without a single word
and detecting this genuine presence in others.

They could reach you more intimately
than even you could yourself.

Today we might consider them primitive,
but maybe they're more human than any of us.

You would have no way of communicating together,
other than those emotions so raw and universal
that even two people with thousands of years separating
their births could recognize in each other.

If these ancestors were here watching your days,
would they see you living authentically?

Words aside.

Would they sense in your eyes, smiles, or fake smiles

that you're living true to yourself,
or for the opinions of others?

I Am

I am no other person,
at no other place,
at no other time.

I am not you.
I am not him.
I am not her.
I am not them.

That is someone else.
This is me.

I am not the me at the market.
I am not the me riding my bike.
I am not the me kissing her.

That was there.
This is here.

I am not the me of tomorrow.
I am not the me of yesterday.

That was then.
This is now.

I am me.
Right here.
Right now.

Your Power

No one has sat on this rock
while writing these words,
thinking these thoughts,
studying that tree with these colorblind eyes,
smiling at this Sun with these teeth.

This moment will never happen again.

They can tell me I'm not special.
They can tell us we aren't worthy.

But I won't believe them.

Mother River

I have two mothers.

One created my body
and one created my soul.
One I knew was my mother from birth
and one I had to remember.
One has been my mother for a lifetime
and one has been my mother since rivers existed.

I didn't even know I was searching for her.
I didn't even know she was out there to be found,
but she was calling for me this whole time.

I spent my summers with her,
catching frogs hiding in her arms.
I felt most loved these warm months
and now I know why.

I began to see myself in her slow nature.
I saw how she embraced change
and I wanted to be like her.

I felt her cleansing touch
and knew she was part of me.
How could she be so strong,
yet so gentle?

I heard her voice and knew it as my bedtime song.
This trickling voice became my favorite sound
on our planet.

She sounded the prettiest where she had

the most obstacles.
I couldn't believe my heart when I realized this.

I wanted to cry.

Then I wanted to cry again,
because crying would bring her out in me.
Every time I feel enough to cry,
she's the first one there.

She is my tears.
How lucky am I?

I must have been a young river in a past life.
A small but vital piece of her waters
that wrap the planet like a giant hug.

Part of me is still in there.
A single drop of water in her waves.

Organic Humans

Here's to you authentic humans
who grow how you want,
not how you're expected.

We need you.
Our world needs you.

There are obstacles in place
keeping you from your unfiltered self.

You will be bothered by weeds.
You will be tempted to take shortcuts.
You will not look how you're told to look.

But the harvest of your organic self.
Oh, I hope you know,
you could feed a village.

Release

Sit down.

I'm not sure how to tell you this,
but I have good news.

You aren't perfect.

What a relief!

Harvesting Balance

Earthly Reminders

When I feel unappreciated,
the air reminds me that some of life's treasures go
unnoticed.

When I'm unsure which path to take,
the reflection on the river reminds me
either direction has beauty.

When I feel guilty about all the good I have,
the sky reminds me I can share it with the world.

When something ends,
the three-leaf clover reminds me everything has a
beginning, middle, and end.

When patience feels out of reach,
the still moss reminds me I will get there when I'm ready.

When I'm feeling lost,
the chatty birds remind me there are people far and wide
ready to chirp their reassuring words for me.

When life feels too much,
the flooded but thriving tree reminds me
that with some self love, I'll be more than okay.

When life feels too little,
the ants remind me nothing on this planet
is any less than any other.

When I don't know the answer,
the baby birds remind me that we have all been here

and will be here again.

When I'm feeling too much,
the Sun reminds me passion isn't a weakness.

When I want security,
the fish jumping out of the water remind me beauty and
meaning lie in moments, not forevers.

When I'm overwhelmed by the hate in the world,
the bee reminds me to look past the initial sting
and try to understand.

When I'm feeling lonely,
the gravel road reminds me I'm just disconnected
from myself.

When an entire day seems to go badly,
the poison ivy reminds me these "bad" moments
light up the good.

Meeting of the Woods

It's as if the creatures of the woods convene
each time I pass through, to give me what I need.

The plants say,
"He seems a little stressed,
so let's turn an even calmer green today."

The owls say,
"I think he needs something unexpected,
so one of us will fly ahead and wait for him on a branch."

The mosses say,
"I remember he likes us,
so we'll grow especially lush today for him."

The winds say,
"He seems to be stuck in his head,
so we'll be extra breezy to quiet his mind."

The trees say,
"He seems to be imbalanced,
so we'll stand firm and remind him that
balance is his to create."

The wildflowers say,
"We'll lean into his path and show him some rain-soaked
colors he's never seen before."

Keystone Humans

Kids are stomping around the river
catching frogs,
or crayfish,
or monsters.

They don't know what tomorrow is.
All they know is today
and what's right in front of them.

These kids are teaching me without knowing.

Their laughter says,
"Look at this beautiful playground."

Their tears say,
"Let yourself feel."

Their hugs say,
"Trust as much as you can."

They remind us what we've forgotten,
just by being themselves.

Plant Some Joy

Plant yourself some joy.

Please.

It won't grow until you do
and no one can plant it for you.

Add some good stuff
and it will blossom.

Take away some bad stuff
and it will show itself again.

Sustainable Humans

They love themselves,
rather than depend on another's love that may run dry.

They motivate themselves,
rather than need another's approval to keep going.

They create happiness,
rather than hope for it to happen.

They realize they're complete and infinite,
rather than consume another's energy just to feel.

Sustainable humans.

An endangered species.

Passionately at Peace

It's that sweet spot.

That balance
between passion and peace.

Who says you can't have both?

Hemispheres

Earth welcomes the Sun in one hemisphere
and the Moon in the other.

She's burning in her molten core
and freezing on her arctic head.

And she's in balance.

We forget we are just little Earths.
Two sides are within us at any moment.

Never one good or one bad.
Just one this and one that.

Maybe your breath is a smooth river,
while your thoughts have wings and take off
like leaves in the wind.

Maybe your head is a stuffy cloud,
while your feet just want to run off their sunny energy.

Earth's opposing moments make her beautiful and alive.
Let's allow ourselves to be just as much.

Harvesting the Moment

Secret Conversation

Here's to those little moments
that were never captured.

Never written about.
Never painted.
Never photographed.

A secret conversation
between you and the universe.

The Thing to Forget

The thing to remember
is what made you smile.

The thing to forget
is how to smile.

Smile in a new way each day
and each deserving moment.

Days go by,
years happen,
milestones are reached,
but please, don't stop there.

There's this thing that happens
in the space between the breaths.
Between the moments.

Before you realize you're having a moment,
that's the magic.

Before you realize you're smiling,
that's it.

That's real and that's life.

This Place

The bees here trust me,
and I trust them.

The mountains here make me feel small
when I need to feel small,
and big when I need to feel big.

The air here is alive,
unlike that pasteurized city air.

The birds here aren't just singing for their love.
They're singing for us all.

The trees here are a green that can only be found
in untouched woods.

The words here flow off my tongue
exactly when and how they're meant to.

The flowers here don't ask to be seen.
They just live their beauty.

The grass here lives every moment in gratitude
for being allowed to grow true.

The families here are more than who you created
or were created from.

The homes here are extensions
of the forests they were built from.

The rain here is more satisfied

because it's giving to Mother Earth,
not manicured lawns.

The quiet here is a quiet that fills you up.

Will it Last?

The relationship.
The love.
The joy.

When it all seems too good,
I welcome the rain to remind me of life's balance.

Will it last?

I ask again and again,
but each time the answer becomes less important.

Dwelling on the day our love might fade
will rob us of something beautiful.
Dwelling on the day the Sun dies
will rob Mother Earth of a life that embraces all life.

Appreciate it all as it is,
in each moment.

That's it.
That's all there is.
That's all I need.

All Too Special

I'm not sure what this life is all about,
but maybe it's these magical little moments.

Like waking up with a smile next to an authentic soul.

Like peeking out of bed
just as the Sun peeks over the treetops.

Like sitting on dewy grass
and trusting everything, if only for a second.

Like moments that are only justified by silence,
because words couldn't touch their beauty.

Like meeting a new human
who knows the same life dance as you.

Like moments of calm where hunger, fear, and pain
escape from your vocabulary.

Like a meal you've had many times,
but the view and company make it all too special.

Lost or Found?

Let the search
be such an adventure
that you no longer
want an answer.

Lesson from a Butterfly

I saw him there with his broken wing,
as if he were ready to die.

Oh, was I wrong.

Before soaring off into the hills, he told me,
"Spend each day dancing around like it's your last,
even if you're less than perfect."

Manifest

Expect magic
and you get magic.

The Unexpected Smile

Instead of counting our smiles.
Instead of counting our moments.

Let's be too busy living
to think about competing with life.

Little Moments

A walk through the woods without words.
A fallen tree that never stopped living.
A slip into a creek that brings more smiles than frowns.
A secret spot not even the rain can drive you from.
A rotting log that's your balancing beam.
A smile that brightens the whole forest.
A leaf's final adventure.

You are Today

May your todays be gracious.
May your yesterdays be what they are.
May your tomorrows be more than you hoped.

Remember,
yesterday's door opens after life,
tomorrow's door may be opened too soon,
but today's door opens with life.

Be careful not to run before you're ready.
Be careful not to wish until you've appreciated.

Today will miss you.

Harvesting Love

Catching Feelings

It's like walking into a forest of towering redwoods,
and only feeling the presence of one.

It's like a dandelion seed floating in the wind,
knowing it's headed somewhere magical,
but the destination is a surprise.

It's like jumping from a cliff into a forbidden lake,
not knowing if it will cleanse you or leave you broken,
but you can't help leaping anyway.

It's like the healing powers
of all the gemstones combined,
existing in that time and space when you're together.

It's like seeing a storm on the horizon,
but instead of running,
you play in the mud and create soggy memories together.

It's like tasting an exotic fruit
and not caring where it came from,
because it alone is enough.

It's like a sacred song,
and only you two know the words.

Sun and Moon

Let's create something so real
that it makes the Sun
fall back in love with the Moon
each time we kiss.

Universal Love

I don't want a girl who loves me more than anything.
I want a girl who loves the world more than anything.

If you're only in love with me,
you're only loving part of me.

I am not just this body and this mind.
It's all me and it's all her.

Love the world,
then you can love me.

I'm part of this world,
so I won't be jealous.

Love Mountain

I've never been up this high before.
She has me on the highest mountain.

I'm not afraid of these emotional heights,
but I am afraid of falling
back down to the everyday ground.

The air up here is fresh,
healing,
exciting.
It's almost too much.

What if I fall off the mountain and lose it all?
I've had a taste of the air,
the treetops,
the clouds.

I'd like to live up here,
but I know I can't.
Life can't be sustained up here forever,
and that's its magic.

I'll savor this blissful mountain air
as long as it will have me.

She helped me up here,
and I'll be forever grateful.

I only hope she's found her own mountain.

Thank You for the Real

What happens when something imaginary
becomes something real?
Was it real the whole time?

Maybe.
Maybe not.
I don't really care.

When something beautiful and real happens.

Just be.
Just feel it.
Just live.

It's real in that moment,
so cherish it for that.

A glimpse into something real,
and I mean something raw,
is a glimpse at God herself.

Harvesting Unity

Our Power

Each time
someone thinks the world
is beautiful and good,
the world becomes
a little more
beautiful and good.

Boundless Family

Family is everywhere.

It's not bound by the language you speak.
Or whether you say "hi" with one syllable or two.
Or whether you eat with your hands or feet.
Or whether you walk on two legs or twelve.
Or whether you grew in a womb or the dirt.
Or the location of your house.
Or the things that make you smile.
Or the things that make you cry.

Family is a feeling
and the only limitations are those we allow.

Loneliness, You're a Fraud

Loneliness is real,
but she's a fraud.

She tricks us into believing her.
I've never truly been alone,
only felt alone.

I forgot everything is alive.
I forgot everything flows with everything else.
I forgot we're all one interspecies family
pouring into each other.

Every second something gives and someone takes,
and it's good.

From up to down.
From hot to cold.
From sad to happy.
From bored to passionate.

The snowflake that landed on my nose
out of countless others.
It chose to share its final moments with me.
How could I feel lonely?

The instrument at the music shop I had to play.
It felt we could be good together.
How could I feel lonely?

The butterfly who kept landing on my shoulders.
He chose to share moments out of his week-long life
with me.

How could I feel lonely?

The apple that fell from its home just as I walked by.
It wanted to meet my taste buds.
How could I feel lonely?

It's all flowing and it's all life.

A Smile

It's a dandelion.
At its release,
it sprinkles seeds all around.

It's an apple tree.
When you feed it,
it feeds others.

It's a sunflower.
At times,
it needs to be cultivated.

It's a wild fern.
Other times,
it pops up on its own.

Our Sun

Her "good morning" rivals any other.
She's there for early morning chats.
She gives everything, but expects nothing.
She knows the value of silence.
She seeks to benefit the world each day.
She says the most beautiful goodbyes.

The Lost Language

She misses us.
Our Mother Earth.
How could we forget her?

We've lost our ears.
Our eyes.
Our Eye.

She sees us listening,
but not to her wind.
She sees us looking,
but not at her changing leaves.

We no longer understand her language.
The universal language.

If we can't connect with her,
how will we understand each other?
How will we protect her if we no longer know her voice?
Her face?

We've forgotten what to look for.
Things have clouded our sight.

We want everything now,
but we don't know how to live now.

Her skies weep for us,
hoping we find our way back.

Back to the center.
Back to life.

Our Mother is showing us the way.

Let's listen.
Let's watch.
Let's learn.

It starts with me.
It starts with you.
It starts with we.

About the Author

Joey Doherty, MA, LPC, CWC is a licensed professional counselor and certified wellness counselor. He graduated from The Ohio State University with a master's in mental health counseling and bachelor's in psychology. Joey has given lectures about self-love, nature deficit disorder, compassion fatigue, natural stress management, meditation, and holistic wellness. He currently lives in Columbus, Ohio.

Website
www.joeydoherty.weebly.com

Instagram
@joeydoherty

Made in USA - North Chelmsford, MA
1024263_9781544773995
11.15.2019 1715